Life is Funny: Poems on Love, Hurt, and Healing

Samantha Rieff

BookLeaf
Publishing

Life is Funny: Poems on Love, Hurt, and Healing © 2023 Samantha Rieff

All rights reserved.

No part of this publication may be reproduced, stored in a retrieval system, or transmitted, in any form or by any means, electronic, mechanical, photocopying, recording or otherwise, without the prior written permission of the presenters.

Samantha Rieff asserts the moral right to be identified as the author of this work.

Presentation by *BookLeaf Publishing*

Web: www.bookleafpub.com

E-mail: info@bookleafpub.com

ISBN: 9789358311341

First edition 2023

*For my dad - Thanks for always rooting for
me, no matter the challenge*

ACKNOWLEDGEMENT

Thank you to my family, Quincy Ham, and my English 2 team for always pushing me to do and be better.

Life is Funny

Life is funny
Sometimes you win
Sometimes you lose
But you always end up where you're supposed to
be

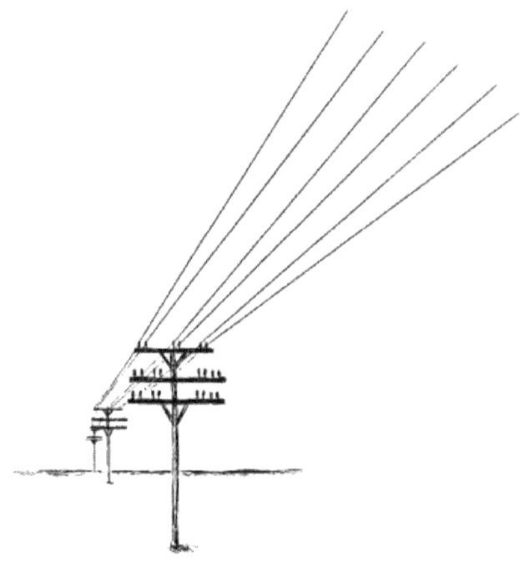

Down

I started on a cruise ship
With many decks
And an endless supply of excitement,
Entertainment,
Enjoyment
Until the first wave hit.

I found myself on a yacht
Still beautiful and elegant
But now I was alone
Alone
Alone
Until the next wave hit.

I was on a rowboat
How did I get here so fast?
How do I make it back to land?
Then the next wave hit.

I drifted on a piece of debris
Maybe I should let go
Maybe this is the time
I felt my arms release the tattered board

Down
        Down
                Down

I wanted to fall
Into the depths
The sandbar stood in my way

This was the sign
There was no other explanation

I need to stay
I need to fight
I'm not done yet

Cliché

How cliché
"Your eyes are like
the stormy sea"

Yet mine, the darkest
shade of brown before
black, get called
"shit"

Why not,
"They're as dark as
the morning coffee that
gives me life"

Or,
"Your eyes are like a
vast forest filled with
mysteries"

And,
"They're a dark
sky on a moonless
night"

I hope

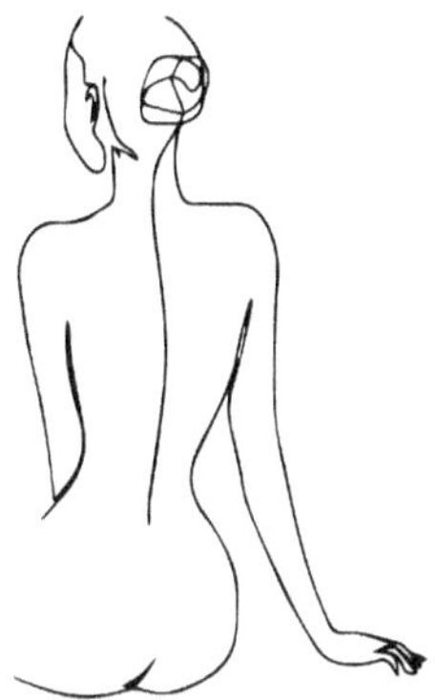

I hope that you learn from every obstacle
I hope that you grow
I hope that you find something that makes life
worth living
I hope that you smile
I hope that you laugh
I hope that you love relentlessly
I hope that you feel
I hope that you cherish
I hope that you get back up every time that you
fall
I hope that you greet each day like a new page in
a book
I hope that you know how much you deserve

Love's Sweet Past

Memories linger, of love's sweet past,
A love so deep, too beautiful to last.
Though you're gone, your mark remains,
In the fragments of love, still it sustains.

I mourn the loss, but I'll rise above,
For love can heal, and hope can prove,
That in time, this pain shall fade,
And in the sun, my heart will pervade.

Though broken now, I'll mend my soul,
And find the strength to be whole.
For love will come, and love will stay,
In a brighter dawn, a brand new day.

Done

One day the sun will rise
And I will smile
No tear rolls down my cheek
But I instinctively wipe it away
Only to realize I was done

9

8

I hope my future husband
Is better than the one in my head
It's a tough act to follow

Wonder

There are days
I sit and wonder
Why I wasn't born
As the lap dog
Of a wealthy family.
Instead I have
To go to work

Crown

Always remember
You wear the most beautiful crown

No matter how you falter
The crown remains

Envy

Everyone always wants what the other has,
Complaining about how green their neighbor's
grass is
But they keep forgetting to water their own
Killing what they should have been cultivating

Sweater

12

Fingers gently weave,
Yarn dances with needles' grace,
A sweater takes form.

Future Daughter

I want my future daughter to be courageous
I want her to look in the face of fear and laugh

I hope that she perseveres
Through whatever sludge she is dumped in

But most of all
I wish my future daughter to be happy

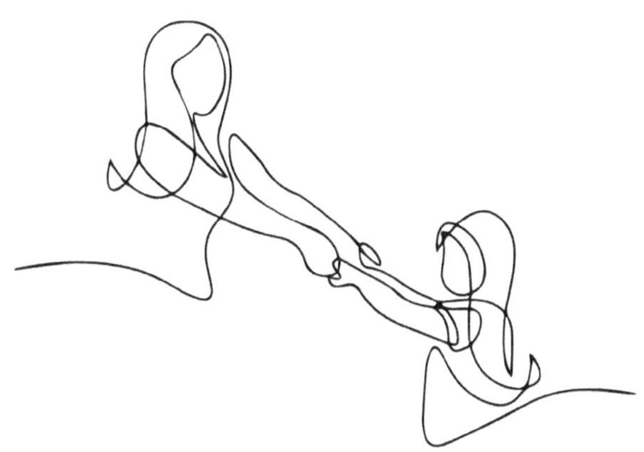

Traffic

If all of traffic
Was caused by ducklings
I would be less mad

Crashing

15

All around me are crashing cars, a chaotic ballet they weave,
They barely miss me as I navigate the road, with heartache on my sleeve,
Sometimes I wish one would sharply turn, fate's hand to swiftly deal,
And end my constant travel, grant respite from life's wheel.

The road stretches on, an endless path, beneath a troubled sky,
Each mile a burden on my soul, as weary days slip by,
In steel and glass, these strangers pass, their lives unknown to me,
Yet in their rush, they fail to see the depths of my decree.

The weight of solitude I bear, like Atlas with his world,
A traveler on this winding course, where destinies are unfurled,
But in the midst of tire and dust, a glimmer of despair,

I seek an end to this endless drive, an answer to
my prayer.

Yet fate, it seems, delights in jest, a puppeteer's
cruel twist,
For when I hope for swift release, the crashes
they persist,
A dance of fate, a tragic waltz, and though I
wish it so,
The twisted irony remains—life's grip won't let
me go.

So I'll press on, amidst the noise, my burden yet
unshaken,
The crashing cars a symphony, my soul forever
taken,
And in the ceaseless traffic's din, I'll find my
solace deep,
For in this constant travel, perhaps, my purpose I
shall reap.

Never Forget

Never forget your worth, she whispered
As she drifted into eternal sleep.
Such strong and powerful words
From a woman who walked through hell and
back
To make sure her family was taken care of
She looked so feeble, so meek, and so fragile
So unfamiliar

Rest easy, because of you I'll never forget

Shadows

In shadows consumed, I lose sight,
A void engulfs, consumed by fear.
I strive to break free, begging for first light,
But darkness lingers, with embracing arms.
When will it end?

My Heart Flew Off a Cliff

It took a leap of faith
Without checking for wings.
Never did it falter
Never did it question
For one word,
One look,
One smile
from you was all it took for
My heart to fly off a cliff.

Kindness

Why are you so kind? They ask
With a quaint sort of disbelief.
Surely someone who has seen so much
Felt so much
Experienced so much
Would be cold and hard.

It's for that reason that I am